Once upon a time, in a little village, there was a Giant's castle. It had a very big garden. There were pretty flowers, tall fruit trees and happy birds.

Every day, the children from the village played in the Giant's garden, but they did not see the Giant.

1

One day the children were in the garden, when they heard a big noise...Boom, Boom, Boom.

They turned and saw a very big pair of boots. They looked up and they saw the Giant's big red face. He was not happy. 'This is *my* garden!' he said.

'These are *my* trees and *my* flowers,' he said, 'and this is *my* castle! It's all mine!'

'This is a very big garden,' a boy said. He pointed to a small corner of the garden. 'Please can we play here? We are very quiet children.'

'NO!' the Giant answered.

The Giant built a big wall around his garden. 'Now the children cannot play in my garden!' he smiled.

He made the wall higher and higher.
'Ha!' he laughed, 'now the children cannot see my garden!'

The children sadly watched the Giant build the wall.

'Oh, he's a selfish Giant!' the children said. 'He has a big and beautiful garden... and we have nothing!'

They watched the Giant build the wall higher and higher. Next, the Giant wrote on the wall. He wrote 'NO CHILDREN' in very big letters.

5

Then it was summer. The children remembered the Giant's garden.

'We were very happy there,' they said.

But summer did not come to the Giant's garden. Every day he looked from his window, and every day it grew colder and cloudier. The garden was very quiet.

The wind came and blew the leaves off the trees.
The snow came, quickly and quietly and all the
flowers went to sleep.

When the thunder and lightning came, the birds
and butterflies were gone. 'My garden is not
beautiful,' the Giant said, 'it's a sad place.'

One day, the Giant put on his big coat and his boots and went into the garden. The wind blew in his face when he walked to the high wall. The snow hurt his cheeks.

The Giant looked over the wall. He was very sad.

'It's sunny over the wall in the village.' he said.

There were leaves on the trees and flowers in the little gardens. It was summer in the village.

'Why did the summer not come to *my* garden?' he asked. 'It's very cold and wintry here.'

9

The children were very sad. They tried to look over the wall around the Giant's garden. But the wall was too high.

'I know...' one boy said, '...we can make a hole in the wall!'

'Brilliant!' the children laughed, and they quickly started to work.

The next morning the Giant heard a little bird singing near his window. He jumped up and looked at the garden.

It was winter in the garden. But in one small corner, near the wall, the Giant could see some flowers and some sun ...and the children.

The children ran from the garden when they saw
the Giant. Winter came again.

'Come back!' the Giant said, 'I'm sorry. It's a sad,
cold place when there are no friends.'

One boy came back into the garden. He was a
very small boy.

'Hello, little friend,' the Giant said.

The Giant smiled and slowly gave his hand. The boy climbed on the Giant's big hand and the Giant put him in the tree. The flowers started to grow and the sun started to smile. The children saw them and they ran happily into the garden.

The children played there every day, but the little boy did not come back.

Years later, when the Giant was old and ill, the little boy came once again.

'You came,' the Giant said.

'Yes,' the little boy answered, 'to say goodbye.'

'Thank you, little friend,' the happy Giant said.

Before You Read

1. Look at the four pictures. Can you find:
   a. spring, **b.** summer, **c.** autumn, **d.** winter?

After You Read

2. Find the children in the pictures.
   a. throwing a snowball. **b.** watching the wind blow.
   c. climbing a tree.   **d.** standing in a tree.

15

Pearson Education Limited

Pearson

KAO Two

KAO Park

Harlow

Essex

CM17 9NA

and Associated Companies throughout the world.

ISBN 9781292240022

This adaptation first published by
Penguin Books 2001

1 3 5 7 9 10 8 6 4 2

Text copyright © Pearson Education Limited 2001
Illustrations copyright © 2001 Richard Hook/Linden Artists; B. Dowty/G-CI

The Selfish Giant © 1888 Oscar Wilde
Adapted by Marie Crook
Series Editor: Melanie Williams
Illustrated by Richard Hook & Bridget Dowty
Design by Rita Storey

Printed in China
SWTC/01

The moral right of the author and illustrator have been asserted

Published by Pearson Education Limited

For a complete list of titles available in the Pearson Story Readers series please write
to your local Pearson Education office or contact:
Pearson, KAO Two, KAO Park, Harlow, Essex, CM17 9NA

Answers for the Activities in this book are published in the free Pearson English Story
Readers Factsheet on the website, www.pearsonenglishreaders.com